Lord, through this hour
Be Thou our Guide,
So by Thy power
No foot shall slide.

Westminster Chimes

A MODERN

Book of Hours

Compiled by Helena T. Olton

Designed by Wulf Stapelfeldt

Published by The C. R. Gibson Company

Norwalk, Connecticut

Special thanks are due
to the members of the staff of the Library of Congress
and of the Alexandria, Virginia, Library
for their unfailing help and courtesy.
H.T.O.

Editorial note:
Scriptural passages from the King James Version
of the Bible are not always given in their entirety.
Points of ellipsis have been omitted in many cases
for greater legibility.

Acknowledgments will be found on pages 118 to 120.

Copyright © MCMLXXIII by
The C. R. Gibson Company, Norwalk, Connecticut
All rights reserved
Printed in the United States of America
Library of Congress Catalog Card Number: 73-78373
ISBN: 0-8378-1861-3

for
JUDY
BRUCE
DAVID
LIBBY
ROB
LIZA
and
MIRANDA

CONTENTS

PAGE		PAGE	
10	Dedication	64	Affirmation
12	Creation	65	Penitence
14	Songs of the Nativity	67	Forgiveness
19	Pilgrims	70	Compassion
21	At Dawning	72	Healing
24	Youth	74	The Seeking Spirit
26	Woman	76	Steadfastness
28	Marriage	78	Renaissance
30	Parenthood	82	Beauty
32	Home	85	Creatures
33	Hospitality	88	Bird Life
38	Work and Effort	90	The Dawn Prayer of the Fisherman
41	Frustration		
42	Choices	92	Shepherds and Sheep
44	Endeavor	94	Aspiration
45	Depression	96	The Soul's Memories
47	Trust	98	Prayer
50	Courage	100	Grace
52	Suffering	102	Joy
54	Guidance	104	Praise
58	Death	106	Blessings
60	Immortality	109	Index
62	Liberation	118	Acknowledgments

Dedication

But be ye doers of the word, and not hearers only.
JAMES 1:22

Now therefore perform the doing of it; that as there was a readiness to will, so there may be a performance also out of that which ye have.
II CORINTHIANS 8:11

THE CELESTIAL SURGEON
If I have faltered more or less
In my great task of happiness;
If I have moved among my race
And shown no glorious morning face;
If beams from happy human eyes
Have moved me not; if morning skies,
Books, and my food, and summer rain
Knocked on my sullen heart in vain: —
Lord, thy most pointed pleasure take
And stab my spirit broad awake.

Robert Louis Stevenson

A PRAYER

We know the paths wherein our feet should press,
   Across our hearts are written Thy decrees;
      Yet now, O Lord, be merciful to bless
         With more than these.

Grant us the will to fashion as we feel,
   Grant us the strength to labour as we know,
      Grant us the purpose, ribb'd and edg'd with steel,
         To strike the blow.

Knowledge we ask not, — knowledge Thou hast lent,
   But, Lord, the will, — there lies our bitter need,
      Guide us to build above the deep intent,
         The deed, the deed.

John Drinkwater

Creation

In the beginning God created the heaven and the earth.
GENESIS 1:1

For we are his workmanship. **EPHESIANS 2:10**

THE SHAPE CALLED STAR

How was it on that day when from His tower
God saw First Land unfolding like a flower?
What was its contour, character and look,
The pristine beauty of the form it took?
Is there no quenching of this vivid thirst
For purest springs, the Origin, the First?
The shape of land in water is Creation,
All land remembers how the world was made
And on each ledge the startled adoration,
The terrifying freshness, still is laid,
Each headland, delta, archipelago
Edged with a line of softly fusing glow;
All coast is stamped with the authentic seal
Of mystery which cannot quite reveal
Something which makes inexplicably sweet
The measured surge where land and water meet.

Louise Townsend Nicholl

Christ keep the Hollow Land
Through the sweet springtide,
When the apple-blossoms bless
The lowly bent hill side.

Christ keep the Hollow Land
All the summertide;
Still we cannot understand
Where the waters glide;

Only dimly seeing them
Coldly slipping through
Many green-lipped cavern mouths
Where the hills are blue.

William Morris

Songs of the Nativity

And she brought forth her first-born son. LUKE 2:7

THE FIRST SUPPER

At the First Supper
The guest were but one.
A maiden was the hostess,
The guest her son.

At the First Supper
No candles were lit;
In darkness hay-scented
They both did sit.

At the First Supper
No table was spread;
In the curve of her elbow
She laid his head.

At the First Supper
They poured no wine;
On milk of the rarest
The guest did dine.

She held him very closely,
Guessing that this
Is the last that any mother
May know of bliss.

Jan Struther

He came all so still
    Where his mother lay
As dew in April
    That falleth on the grass.

He came all so still
    To his mother's bower
As dew in April
    That falleth on the flower.

He came all so still
    Where his mother lay
As dew in April
    That falleth on the spray.

Anonymous, 15th Century

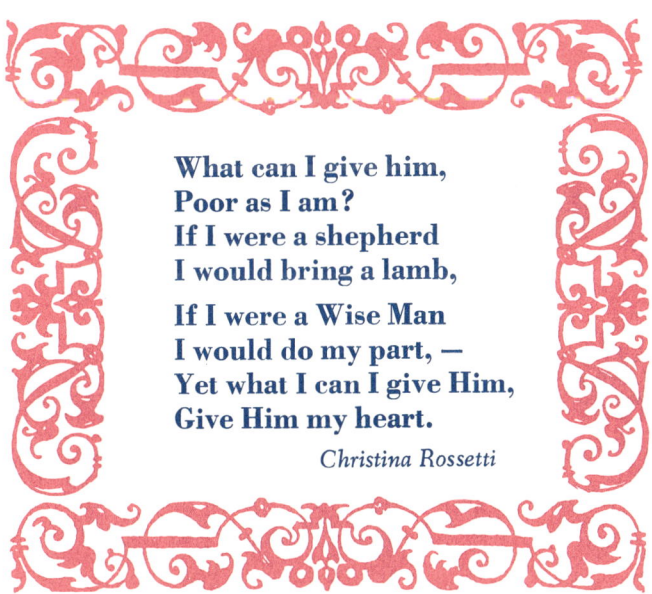

What can I give him,
Poor as I am?
If I were a shepherd
I would bring a lamb,

If I were a Wise Man
I would do my part, —
Yet what I can I give Him,
Give Him my heart.

Christina Rossetti

And the Word was made flesh, and dwelt among us.
JOHN 1:14

ARMENIAN POEM
The lips of the Christ Child are like two twin leaves
That let roses fall when He smiles tenderly;
The tears of the Christ Child are pearls when He grieves;
The eyes of the Christ Child are deep as the sea.
Like pomegranate grains are the dimples He hath,
And clustering lilies spring up in His path.

Christ took our nature on Him, not that He
'Bove all else loved it for its purity;
No — He dressed Him in our human trim because
Our flesh stood most in need of Him.

Robert Herrick

Our Little Lord, we give Thee praise
That Thou hast deigned to take our ways,
Born of a maid, a man to be,
And all the angels sing to Thee.

Martin Luther

. . . and wrapped him in swaddling clothes,
and laid him in a manger.

LUKE 2:7

OLD CAROL
The son of God is born for all
At Beth'lem in a cattle stall;
He lieth in a crib so small,
And wrapt in swaddling clothes withal.

THE CHRIST-CHILD'S LULLABY

My love, my dear, my darling thou,
My treasure new, my gladness thou,
My comely beauteous babe-son thou,
Unworthy I to tend to thee.

Hosanna to the Son of David,
My King, my Lord, and my Saviour!
Great my joy to be song-lulling thee—
Blessed among the women I.

Kenneth Macleod

Help us rightly to remember the birth of Jesus, that we may share in the song of the angels, the gladness of the shepherds, and the worship of the Wise Men.

Robert Louis Stevenson

**May Christ give to us
At this time and for always,
His Peace in our souls,
His Promise in our hearts,
His Power in our lives.**

Dearly beloved, I beseech you as strangers and pilgrims ... I PETER 2:11

—for here we have no continuing city. HEBREWS 13:14

King of the elements, Love, Father of Bliss,
In my pilgrimage from airt to airt,
    From airt to airt,
May each evil be a good to me,
May each sorrow be a gladness to me,
And may Thy son be my foster-brother,
Oh, may Thy son be my foster-brother.

Holy Spirit, Spirit of Light,
A pilgrim I, throughout the night,
    Throughout the night.
Love my heart pure as the stars,
Love my heart pure as the stars,
Nor fear I then the spells of evil,
    The spells of evil.

Jesus, son of the virgin-pure,
Be thou my pilgrim-staff throughout the land.
    Throughout the land.
Thy love in all my thought.
Thy likeness in my face,
May I heart-warm to others and they heart-warm to me,
    For the love of Thee.
    For the love of Thee.

Kenneth Macleod

He who would valiant be
'Gainst all disaster,
Let him in constancy
Follow the Master.
There's no discouragement
Shall make him once relent
His first avowed intent
To be a pilgrim.

John Bunyan

Thou art the comfortable resting-place of the righteous, and Thou enablest them to see Thee. Thou art the Beginning and the End of all things. Thou bearest up all things without effort. Thou art the Way, and the Guide, and the Bourne whither the way leadeth; And to Thee all men are hastening.

Boethius, 6th Century

At Dawning

Cause me to hear thy lovingkindness in the morning.
PSALM 143:8

I arise from rest with movements swift
As the beat of the raven's wings
I arise
To meet the day.
My face is turned from the dark of night
To gaze at the dawn of day
Now whitening in the sky.

From the Eskimo, translated by Knud Rasmussen

New every morning is the love
Our waking and uprising prove;
From sleep and darkness safely brought
Restored to life and power and thought.

John Keble

**At the dawn I seek Thee,
Refuge, Rock Sublime;
Set my prayer before Thee in the morning
and my prayer at eventime.**

Jewish, 11th Century

*Rejoice, O young man, in thy youth;
and let thy heart cheer thee in the days of
thy youth, and walk in the ways of thine heart,
and in the sight of thine eyes.*
ECCLESIASTES 11:9

Let no man despise thy youth.
I TIMOTHY 4:12

*When I was young, every day was as a beginning of some new thing
and every evening ended with the glow of the next day's dawn.*
From the Eskimo, translated by Knud Rasmussen

And as I was green and carefree, famous
   among the barns
About the happy yard and singing as the
   farm was home,
      In the sun that is young once only,
      Time let me play and be
      Golden in the mercy of his means,
And green and golden I was huntsman and
   herdsman, the calves
Sang to my horn, the foxes on the hills
   barked clear and cold,
      And the sabbath rang slowly
      In the pebbles of the holy streams.

Dylan Thomas

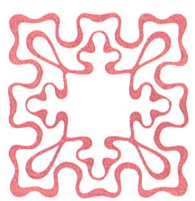

Blesséd Lord, what it is to be young:
To be of, to be for, be among —
   Be enchanted, enthralled,
   Be the caller, the called,
The singer, the song, and the sung.

David McCord

. . . but she hath washed my feet with tears, and wiped them with the hairs of her head.
LUKE 7:44

It was Mary Magdalene, and Joanna, and Mary the mother of James, and other women that were with them, which told these things unto the apostles.
LUKE 24:10

. . . she, supposing him to be the gardener . . .
JOHN 20:15

WOMAN

Not she with traitorous kiss her Saviour stung,
Nor she denied Him with unholy tongue,
She, while apostles shrank, could dangers brave,
Last at the cross and earliest at the grave.

Eaton Stannard Barret

And Mary said, My soul doth magnify the Lord,

And my spirit hath rejoiced in God my Saviour.

For he hath regarded the low estate of his handmaiden: for, behold, from henceforth all generations shall call me blessed.

For he that is mighty hath done to me great things; and holy is his name.

From The Magnificat

Marriage

That the sons of God saw
the daughters of men
that they were fair;
and they took them wives. . . .

GENESIS 6:2

For this cause shall a man leave father
and mother, and shall cleave to his wife:
and they twain shall be one flesh.

MATTHEW 19:5

TRUE LOVE

True love is but a humble, low-born thing,
And hath its food served up in earthenware;
It is a thing to walk with, hand in hand,
Through the everydayness of this work-day world,
Baring its tender feet to every roughness,
Yet letting not one heart-beat go astray
From beauty's law of plainness and content —
A simple, fireside thing, whose quiet smile
Can warm earth's poorest hovel to a home.

James Russell Lowell

TO HIS WIFE

Love, let us live as we have lived, nor lose
   The little names that were the first night's grace,
And never come the day that sees us old,
   I still your lad, and you my little lass.
Let me be older than old Nestor's years,
   And you the Sibyl, if we heed it not.
What should we know, we two, of ripe old age?
   We'll have its richness, and the years forgot.

Ausonius, translated from the Latin by Helen Waddell

Keep us steadfast, O God, in the affections of our hearts that, in our constancy, we may forever be worthy of those who love and trust us.

H.T.O.

Parenthood

For of such is the kingdom of God.
MARK 10:14

WHAT IS A FAMILY?

A family is a single word —
   in the heart heard —
   meaning beyond its syllables,
   its hyphen ties of mother-son,
   father-daughter, miracles
   of loyalty and communion.

Say it and any heart grows firm!
It is a contract, it is a term
   of time that compasses the past
   and finds and makes the future fast —
   a knee to sit on, a head to pat —
   and a natural habitat!

In all you have tried to do, or planned
   it must stand behind you, or offer cheer,
   or hope a little, or lend a hand.
Courage! it cries, There is someone here!

Helen Harrington

Our Father, by whose Name
All fatherhood is known,
Who dost in love proclaim
Each family thine own,
Bless thou all parents, guarding well,
With constant love as sentinel,
The homes in which
thy people dwell.

F. B. Tucker

That our sons may be as
plants grown up in their youth;
that our daughters may be as
corner stones.

PSALM 144:12

Home

Except the Lord build the house, they labour in vain that build it. PSALM 127:1

RUNE OF THE PEAT FIRE
The first layer of peats is laid down
in the name of the God of Life,
the second in the name of the God of Peace,
and the third in the name of
the God of Grace.

THE
SACRED
THREE
To save
To shield,
To surround,
The hearth,
The house,
The household,
This eve,
This night:
Oh, this eve,
This night,
And every night,
Each single night.
Amen.

Kenneth Mcleod

A QUAKER QUERY

Are you endeavoring to make your home a place of friendliness, refreshment, and peace, where God becomes more real to those who dwell therein, and to all who visit there?

Hospitality

And they told . . . how he was known of them in breaking of bread.
LUKE 24:35

Be not forgetful to entertain strangers: for thereby some have entertained angels unawares.
HEBREWS 13:2

Thou shalt neither vex a stranger, nor oppress him: for ye were strangers in the land of Egypt.
EXODUS 22:21

RUNE OF HOSPITALITY

I saw a stranger yestre'en
Put food in the eating place
Drink in the drinking place
Music in the listening place.

And in the sacred name of the Triune
He blessed myself and my house,
My cattle and my dear ones.

And the lark sang in her song,
    Often, often, often,
Goes the Christ in stranger's guise,
    Often, often, often,
Goes the Christ in stranger's guise.

Kenneth Macleod

**Reveal Thy presence now, O Lord,
As in the upper room of old;
Break Thou our bread,
Grace Thou our board,
And keep our hearts from growing cold.**

Old Prayer

**O God, whose blessed Son did manifest himself
to his disciples in the breaking of bread;
open, we pray thee, the eyes of our faith,
that we may behold thee in all thy works.
Amen.**

Book of Common Prayer

Love ye therefore the stranger: for ye were strangers in the land of Egypt. DEUTERONOMY 10:19

When saw we thee a stranger, and took thee in?
MATTHEW 25:38

The lands around my dwelling
Are more beautiful
From the day
When it is given me to see
Faces I have never seen before.
All is more beautiful,
All is more beautiful,
And life is Thankfulness.
These guests of mine
Make my house grand.

From the Eskimo, translated by Knud Rasmussen

**As the fire under the stone floor * * *
of my dwelling place burns brightly to
warm my house, so may the love of God warm my
heart and the hearts of those
who step over my threshold.**

Formosan Prayer

Work and Effort

*Blessed is every one that feareth the Lord . . .
For thou shalt eat the labour of thine hands:
happy shalt thou be, and it shall be
well with thee.*

PSALM 128 : 1,2

THE RUNE OF THE WEAVER

    O Loom of Love,
    Weave thy Rune;
    Loom of Love by lone waves,
    Weave thy Rune.

Thou art the laughter, thou art the tears,
O Rune by the lone waves woven,
Thou art the song, and thou art the pain,
O Rune by lone waves woven.

    O Loom of Love,
    Weave thy Rune;
    Loom of Love by lone waves,
    O Loom of Love.
    Weave thy Rune,
    By lone waves,
    Weave, weave.

Kenneth Mcleod

THE BOY WITH THE CART

In our fields, fallow and burdened, in grass and furrow,
In barn and stable, with scythe, flail, or harrow,
Sheepshearing, milking or mowing, on labour that's older
Than knowledge, with God we work shoulder to shoulder.

Christopher Fry

> **And let the beauty of the Lord our God be upon us: and establish thou the work of our hands upon us; yea, the work of our hands establish thou it.**
>
> **PSALM 90:17**

*. . . and every man shall receive
his own reward according to his own labour.
For we are labourers together with God.
Every man's work shall be made manifest.
If any man's work abide which he hath built
thereupon, he shall receive a reward.*

I CORINTHIANS 3:8,9,13,14

DAILY LIVING

The ample busyness of life went by,
All the full busyness of lives
Unknown to fame, made lovely by no words;
The shepherd lonely in the winter fold;
The tiller following the eternal plough
Beneath a stormy or a gentle sky;
The sower with his gesture like a gift
Walking the furrowed hill from base to brow;
The reaper in the piety of thrift
Binding the sheaf against his slanted thigh.

V. Sackville—West

THE MONK IN THE KITCHEN

Whoever makes a thing more bright,
He is an angel of all light.
When I cleanse this earthen floor
My spirit leaps to see
Bright garments trailing over it,
A cleanness made by me.

Whoever makes a thing more bright
He is an angel of all light.
Therefore, let me spread abroad
The beautiful cleanness of my God.

Anna Hempstead Branch

**Teach me, my God and King,
In all things thee to see,
And what I do in any thing,
To do it as for thee.** *George Herbert*

Frustration

For to will is present with me; but how to perform that which is good I find not. ROMANS 7:18

There was given to me a thorn in the flesh. . . .
II CORINTHIANS 12:7

I wonder why
My song-to-be that I wish to use,
My song-to-be that I wish to put together,
I wonder why it will not come to me.
At Sioraq it was at a fishing hole in the ice,
I could feel a little trout on the line,
And then it was gone.
I stood jigging.
But why is it so difficult, I wonder?
When summer came and the waters opened,
It was then that catching became so hard;
I am not good at hunting!
            C. M. Bowra

O God, whose eternal might doth undergird our insufficiency, help us to trust in Thee when we are shaken and uncertain. Take away our needless fears, lighten our confusions, and give us such strength as shall enable us to meet steadily whatever the day may hold; through the grace and power of Thy Holy Spirit.

How long halt ye between two opinions?
I KINGS 18:21

No man can serve two masters.
MATTHEW 6:24

*Seek ye first the kingdom of God,
and his righteousness.*
MATTHEW 6:33

MAN TEST
I will leave man to make the fateful guess,
Will leave him torn between the No and Yes,
Leave him unresting till he rests in Me,
Drawn upward by the choice that makes him free —
Leave him in tragic loneliness to choose,
With all in life to win or all to lose.
               Edwin Markham

Thou hast made us for Thyself, O God,
and our hearts are restless until
they rest in Thee.

St. Augustine

THE WASTE LAND

There shall always be the Church, and the World,
And the heart of man
Shivering and fluttering between
Them, choosing and chosen
Valiant, ignoble, dark, and full of light
Swinging between hell gate and heaven gate
And the gates of hell shall not prevail.

T. S. Eliot

Oh God, who seest that of ourselves we have no strength, keep us both outwardly and inwardly that we may be defended from all adversities which may happen to the body and from all evil thoughts which may assault and hurt the soul;

Book of Common Prayer

Endeavor

Say not ye, There are yet four months, and then cometh the harvest? behold, I say unto you, Lift up your eyes, and look on the fields; for they are white already to harvest.

JOHN 4:35

With him are the keys of the unseen.
He it is who takes you to himself and knows
What ye have gained in the day:
Then he raises you up again, that your
Appointed time may be fulfilled: then unto
Him is your return, and then he will
Inform you of what you have done.

The Koran

What hath this day deserved?
    What hath it done
That it in golden letters should be set
Among the high tides in the calendar?

William Shakespeare

O Lord God, when Thou givest to Thy servants to endeavor any great matter, grant us also to know that it is not the beginning, but the continuing of the same, until it be thoroughly finished which yieldeth the true glory.

Sir Francis Drake

Depression

How shall we sing the Lord's song in a strange land? PSALM 137:4

Why art thou cast down, O my soul? and why art thou disquieted in me? PSALM 42:5

If therefore the light that is in thee be darkness, how great is that darkness! MATTHEW 6:23

A SONG IN TIME OF DEPRESSION
From the Paiute

Now all my singing Dreams are gone
But none knows where they are fled
Nor by what trail they have left me.
Return, O Dreams of my heart,
And sing in the summer twilight,
By the creek and the almond thicket
And the field that is bordered with lupine!

Now is my refuge to seek
In the hollow of friendly shoulders,
Since the singing is stopped in my pulse
And the earth and the sky refuse me;
Now must I hold by the eye of a friend
When the high white stars are unfriendly.

Oversweet is the refuge of trusting;
Return and sing, O my Dreams,
In the dewy and palpitant pastures,
Till the love of living awakes
And the strength of the hills to uphold me.

George W. Cronyn

I have been one acquainted with the night,
I have walked out in rain — and back in rain.
I have outwalked the furthest city light.
I have been one acquainted with the night.

Robert Frost

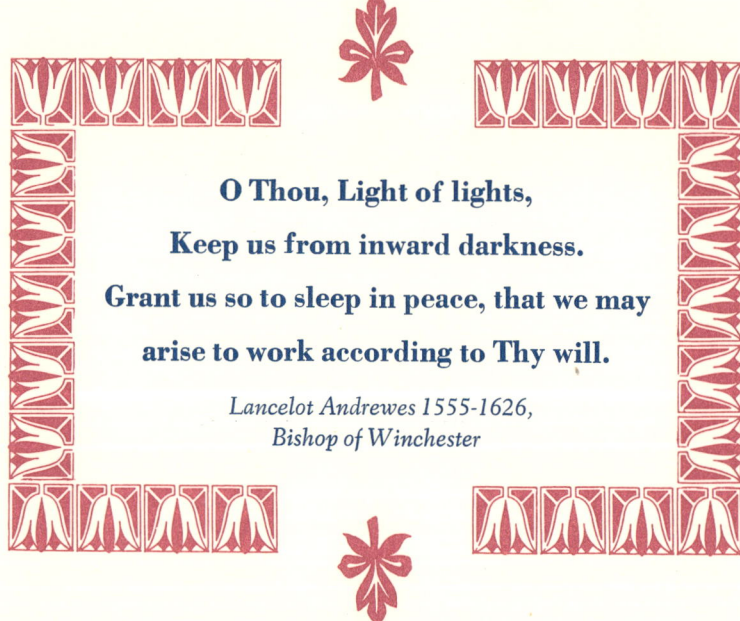

O Thou, Light of lights,
Keep us from inward darkness.
Grant us so to sleep in peace, that we may
arise to work according to Thy will.

*Lancelot Andrewes 1555-1626,
Bishop of Winchester*

Lighten our darkness, we beseech thee, O Lord;
and by thy great mercy defend us from all perils
and dangers of this night; for the love of thy
only Son, our Saviour, Jesus Christ.
Amen.

Book of Common Prayer

I will stand upon my watch, and set me upon the tower, and will watch to see what he will say unto me, and what I shall answer . . .

HABAKKUK 2:1

For thou hast delivered my soul from death, mine eyes from tears, and my feet from falling.

PSALM 116:8

Let nothing disturb thee:
Nothing affright thee;
All things are passing;
God never changeth;
Patient endurance
Attaineth to all things:
Who God possesseth
In nothing is wanting:
Alone God sufficeth.

St. Theresa

What else is Wisdom,
What of man's endeavor,
Or God's high grace, so lovely and so great —
To stand from fear set free,
To breathe and wait . . . .
Euripides

O Lord God, who seest that we put not our trust in any thing that we do; Mercifully grant that by thy power we may be defended against all adversity, through Jesus Christ our Lord.

Book of Common Prayer

*The eternal God is thy refuge,
and underneath are
the everlasting arms.*
DEUTERONOMY 33:27

*Behold, I have taken out of thine hand
the cup of trembling, thou shalt no more
drink it again.*
ISAIAH 51:22

THE RUNE OF ST. PATRICK

At Tara today in this fateful hour
I place all Heaven with its power,
And the sun with its brightness,
And the snow with its whiteness,
And fire with all the strength it hath,
And lightning with its rapid wrath,
And the winds with their swiftness
   along their path,
And the sea with its deepness,
And the rocks with their steepness,
And the earth with its starkness;
All these I place,
By God's almighty help and grace
Between myself and the powers
   of darkness.

From the Old Gaelic

Lord, when I look upon mine own life it seems Thou hast led me so carefully, so tenderly, Thou canst have attended to no one else; but when I see how wonderfully Thou hast led the world and art leading it, I am amazed that Thou hast time to attend to such as I.

St. Augustine

Courage

Be strong and of a good courage; be not afraid, neither be thou dismayed: for the Lord thy God is with thee whithersoever thou goest.
JOSHUA 1:9

And none shall make him afraid.
JEREMIAH 30:10

I can do all things through Christ which strengtheneth me.
PHILIPPIANS 4:13

I bind unto myself this day
The virtues of the star-lit heaven,
The glorious sun's life-giving ray,
The whiteness of the moon at even,
The flashing of the lightning free,
The whirling wind's tempestuous shocks,
The stable earth, the deep salt sea,
Around the old eternal rocks.

I bind unto myself today
The power of God to hold and lead,
His eyes to watch, his might to stay,
His ear to hearken to my need;
The wisdom of my God to teach,
His hand to guide, his shield to ward;
The word of God to give me speech
His heavenly host to be my guard.

St. Patrick

Of wounds and sore defeat
I made my battle stay;
Wingéd sandals for my feet
I wove of my delay;
Of weariness and fear,
I made my shouting spear;
Of loss, and doubt, and dread,
And swift oncoming doom
I made a helmet for my head
And a floating plume.

William Vaughn Moody

When to danger duty calls me,
And grave peril then befalls me,
Gird me, guard me, guide me safely,
  Till from danger I am free.

Should my courage seem to fail me,
When, with fierceness foes assail me,
Gird me, guard me, guide me safely,
  Till from danger I am free,
Guard me, guide Thou me.

Gioacchino Rossini

Suffering

As ye are partakers of the sufferings, so shall ye be also of the consolation.   II CORINTHIANS 1:7

THE TEN PAINS OF DEATH

To wait for one who never comes,
To lie in bed and not to sleep,
To serve well and not to please,
To have a horse that will not go,
To be sick and lack the cure,
To be a prisoner without hope,
To lose the way when you would journey,
To stand at a door that none will open,
To have a friend who would betray you,
These are the ten pains of death.

Giovanni Florio, 1591

Nobody knows the trouble I've seen —
Nobody knows but Jesus —

Negro Spiritual

O God, Author of the world's joy,
Bearer of the world's pain; at the heart
of all our troubles and sorrow let
unconquerable gladness dwell.

These tears that dim my eyes,

This pain that plows my heart;

Take them, Lord, I give them Thee

As I give my gaiety.

Only let me keep as mine

The blessing that is here;

So to others I may be

Always warm with sympathy.

Anonymous

Guidance

*Thy word is a lamp unto my feet,
and a light unto my path.*
PSALM 119:105

I am the light of the world.
JOHN 8:12

And I said to the man who stood at the
  gate of the year
"Give me a light that I may tread safely
  into the unknown:"
And he replied,
"Go out into the darkness and put thine
  hand into the hand of God. That
shall be to thee better than any light and
  safer than any known way."

M. L. Haskins

Thou one all perfect light;
Our lamps are lit at Thine;
And into darkness, as of night,
We go, to prove they shine.

M. Elizabeth Crouse

**Bestow Thy light upon us, O Lord,
so that being rid of the darkness of
our hearts, we may attain unto the true Light;
through Jesus Christ, who is the Light
of the world.**

Sarum Breviary

**Keep thou my feet; I do not ask to see
The distant scene; one step enough
for me.**

John Henry Newman

Death

Lord, remember me when thou comest into thy kingdom.

LUKE 23 : 42

THE DEATH CROON

Home thou'rt going tonight to the Winter Ever-house
The Autumn, Summer, and Springtide Ever-house,
Home art going tonight on music of cantors,
White angels wait thee on the shores of the Avon.

> God the Father with thee in sleep
> Jesus Christ with thee in sleep,
> God the Spirit with thee in sleep.
> Softly sleep, softly sleep.

In the name of the Three in One, Peace to thy pain,
The Christ is come, thou'rt at peace from all pain,
O the Christ is come, thou'rt at peace from all pain.

> Softly to sleep, softly to sleep,
> Softly to sleep, softly to sleep.

From the Gaelic

Lord, now lettest thou thy servant depart in peace, . . . for mine eyes have seen thy salvation.

LUKE 2:29-30

Father, into Thy hands I commend my spirit.

LUKE 23:46

Immortality

I am he that liveth, and was dead; and, behold
I am alive forevermore.
REVELATION 1:18

I will behold thy face in righteousness:
I shall be satisfied, when I awake,
with thy likeness.
PSALM 17:15

I am the resurrection, and the life. JOHN 11:25

DEATH BE NOT PROUD

Death, be not proud, though some have called thee
Mighty and dreadful, for thou art not so,
For those whom thou think'st thou dost overthrow
Die not, poor death, nor yet canst thou kill me.

John Donne

For this corruptible must put on incorruption,
and this mortal must put on immortality.
So when this corruptible shall have put on incorruption,
and this mortal shall have put on immortality,
then shall be brought to pass the saying that is written,
Death is swallowed up in victory.
O death, where is thy sting?
O grave, where is thy victory? . . .
Thanks be to God, which giveth us the victory. . . .

         I CORINTHIANS 15:53-57

O Lord, support us all the day long, until the shadows lengthen and the evening comes, and the busy world is hushed, and the fever of life is over, and our work is done. Then in thy mercy grant us a safe lodging, and a holy rest, and peace at the last.

John Henry Newman

Liberation

For, brethren, ye have been called unto liberty.
GALATIANS 5:13

Because the creature itself also shall be delivered . . . into the glorious liberty of the children of God. ROMANS 8:21

OF SIMPLE SIGNIFICANCE

O Blessed Trinity,
O Holy Mystery, One God,
Set us free.

When our lives are chained
To insignificance,
How shall we move into
Your loving Light?
We beseech you, Lord, set us free.

When our love is chained
To selfishness,
How shall we ever know
The gallantry of
Your gay Selflessness?
We beseech you, Lord, set us free.

When our minds are chained
To thoughtlessness,
How shall we escape
To the bright spontaneity
Of Your Eternity?
We beseech you, Lord, set us free.

When our souls are chained
To pettiness,
How shall we liberate them
To your Joyous Peace?
We beseech you, Lord, set us free.

Kay Smallzried

Affirmation

I will go in the strength of the Lord God.
PSALM 71:16

TOMORROW I SHALL BEND THE BOW

Tomorrow I shall bend the bow,
My soul shall have her mark again,
My bosom feel the archer's strain.

No longer pacing to and fro
With idle hands and listless brain,
As goes the arrow, forth I go.

My soul shall have her mark again,
My bosom feel the archer's strain,
Tomorrow I shall bend the bow

Padraic Colum

NAVAJO CHANT

My body restore thou for me,
My mind restore thou for me.
My voice restore thou for me.
Restore all for me in beauty.
Make beautiful all that is before me,
Make beautiful all that is behind me,
It is done in beauty.
It is done in beauty.

George W. Cronyn

Penitence

Have mercy upon me, O God, according to thy lovingkindness: according unto the multitude of thy tender mercies blot out my transgressions. Wash me thoroughly from mine iniquity, and cleanse me from my sin. PSALM 51:1,2

At the round earth's imagined corners, blow
Your trumpets, Angels, and arise, arise
From death, you numberless infinities
Of souls, and to your scattered bodies go,
All whom the flood did, and fire shall o'erthrow,
All whom war, dearth, age, agues, tyrannies,
Despaire, law, chance, hath slaine, and you whose eyes
Shall behold God, and never taste death's woe,

But let them sleep, Lord, and me mourne a space,
For, if above all these, my sinns abound,
'Tis late to ask abundance of thy grace
When we are there; here on this lowly ground,
Teach me how to repent; for that's as Good
As if Thou hadst sealed my pardon with Thy Blood.

John Donne

THE EVERLASTING MERCY

O Christ who holds the open gate,
O Christ who drives the furrow straight,
O Christ, the plough, O Christ, the laughter
Of holy white birds, flying after.
Lo, all my heart's field red and torn,
And Thou wilt bring the young green corn
The young green corn divinely springing
The young green corn for ever singing;
The corn that makes the holy bread
By which the soul of man is fed,
The holy bread, the food unpriced,
Thy everlasting mercy, Christ.

John Masefield

THE GRACE TO BEGIN AGAIN

**O forgiving Father, who never wearieth of
our repentance: Grant that we may constantly
lay hold of thy everlasting mercy
and so obtain the grace
to begin once more.**

Gerald Heard (adapted)

Forgiveness

Bless the Lord, O my soul, and forget not all his benefits: Who forgiveth all thine iniquities; who healeth all thy diseases. PSALM 103:2,3

Father, forgive them; for they know not what they do. LUKE 23:34

 LOVE

Love bade me welcome; yet my soul drew back,
    Guilty of dust and sin.
But quick-eyed Love, observing me grow slack
    From my first entrance in,
Drew nearer to me, sweetly questioning
    If I lacked anything.
A guest, I answered, worthy to be here.
    Love said, You shall be he.
I, the unkind, ungrateful? Ah, my dear,
    I cannot look on Thee.
Love took my hand, and smiling, did reply,
    Who made the eyes but I?
Truth, Lord, but I have marred them: let my shame
    Go where it doth deserve.
And know you not, says Love, who bore the blame?
    My dear, then I will serve.
You must sit down, says Love, and taste my meat.
    So I did sit and eat.
              George Herbert

Forgive us our trespasses, as we forgive those that trespass against us. Amen.

Compassion

But the fruit of the Spirit is love, joy, peace, longsuffering, gentleness, goodness, faith, meekness, temperance.

GALATIANS 5: 22,23

THE DIVINE IMAGE

To Mercy, Pity, Peace, and Love
All pray in their distress;
And to these virtues of delight
Return their thankfulness.

For Mercy, Pity, Peace, and Love
Is God, our Father dear,
And Mercy, Pity, Peace, and Love
Is Man, His child and care.

For Mercy has a human heart,
Pity a human face,
And Love, the human form divine,
And Peace, the human dress.

Then every man, of every clime,
That prays in his distress,
Prayer to the human form divine,
Love, Mercy, Pity, Peace.

All must love the human form,
In heathen, Turk, or Jew;
Where Mercy, Love, and Pity dwell
There God is dwelling too.

William Blake

There is no such thing as humanity. What we call humanity
has a name, was born, lives on a street, gets hungry,
needs all the particular things we need.
As an abstract, it has no reality whatsoever.

Howard Thurman

**Lord, who has form'd me out of mud,
And has redeem'd me through thy blood,
And sanctifi'd me to do good;**

**Purge all my sins done heretofore;
For I confess my heavy score,
And I will strive to sin no more.**

**Enrich my heart, mouth, hands in me,
With faith, with hope, with charity,
That I may run, rise, rest with thee.**

George Herbert

Healing

*But the Comforter,
. . . whom the Father will send in my name,
he shall teach you all things. . . .*

JOHN 14:26

*I say unto thee, Arise, and take up thy couch
and go into thine house.*

LUKE 5:24.

WHITSUNTIDE

O Holy Spirit of great power,
Come down upon us and subdue us;
From Thy glorious mansion in the heavens
Thy light effulgent shed on us.

Father beloved of every naked one,
From Whom all gifts and goodness come,
Our hearts illumine with Thy mercy,
In Thy mercy shield us from all harm.

The knee that is stiff; O Healer, make pliant,
The heart that is hard make warm beneath Thy wing;
The soul that is wandering from Thy path,
Grasp Thou his helm and he shall not die.

Each thing that is foul cleanse Thou each,
Each thing that is hard soften Thou with Thy grace,
Each wound that is working as pain
O best of healers, make Thou whole!

Translation of a traditional Gaelic hymn

O living Christ, make us conscious of Thy healing nearness. Touch our eyes that we may see Thee, open our ears that we may hear Thy voice; enter our hearts that we may know Thy love. Overshadow our souls and bodies with Thy presence that we may partake of Thy strength, Thy love and Thy healing life.

Howard Chandler Robbins

The Seeking Spirit

Seek ye the Lord while he may be found, call ye upon him while he is near.

ISAIAH 55:6

Blessed are they which do hunger and thirst after righteousness.

MATTHEW 5:6

Whose is the voice that will not let me rest?
   I hear it speak.
Where is the shore will gratify my quest,
   Show what I seek?
Whose is the loveliness I know is by,
   Yet cannot place?
Is it perfection of the sea or sky,
   Or human face?
Whose are the feet that pass me, echoing on
   unknown ways?
Whose are the lips that only part to sing
   Through all my days?

Anonymous

Who reads the verse I write
Shall know the falcon's flight,
The vision single and sure, the conquest of air and sun!
Is there aught else worthy to weave within your
    banners' folds?
Is there aught else worthy to grave on the blade
    of your naked swords?

Padraic Colum

Teach me to hear Mermaids singing,

Or to keep off envy's stinging,

And find

What wind

Serves to advance an honest mind.

John Donne

Steadfastness

Let a man so account of us, as of the ministers of Christ, and stewards of the mysteries of God. Moreover it is required in stewards, that a man be found faithful.

I CORINTHIANS 4:1-2

Let me not to the marriage of true minds
Admit impediments. Love is not love
Which alters when it alteration finds,
Or bends with the remover to remove:
O, no! it is an ever-fixéd mark,
That looks on tempests and is never shaken;
It is the star to every wandering bark,
Whose worth's unknown, although his height be taken,
Love's not Time's fool, though rosy lips and cheeks
Within his bending sickle's compass come;
Love alters not with his brief hours and weeks,
But bears it out even to the edge of doom.
If this be error, and upon me proved,
I never writ, nor no man ever loved.

William Shakespeare, Sonnet 116

O Lord of the vineyard, we beg Thy blessing upon all who truly desire to serve Thee by being diligent and faithful in their several callings, bearing their due share of the world's burden, and going about their daily tasks in all simplicity and uprightness of heart.

John Baillie

Renaissance

Except a man be born again, he cannot see the kingdom of God. JOHN 3:3

He hath put a new song in my mouth. PSALM 40:3

THE FLOWER

How fresh, O Lord, how sweet and clean
Are Thy returns! Ev'n as the flowers in spring,
   To which, besides their own demean,
The late-past frosts tributes of pleasure bring.
     Grief melts away
     Like snow in May,
As if there were no such cold thing.

   Who would have thought my shrivel'd heart
Could have recover'd greenness? It was gone
   Quite underground, as flowers depart
To see their mother-root when they have blown;
     Where they together
     All the hard weather,
Dead to the world, keep house unknown.

   And now in age I bud again,
After so many deaths, I live and write;
   I once more smell the dew and rain,
And relish versing. O my only light,
     It cannot be
     That I am he
On whom thy tempests fell at night.

George Herbert

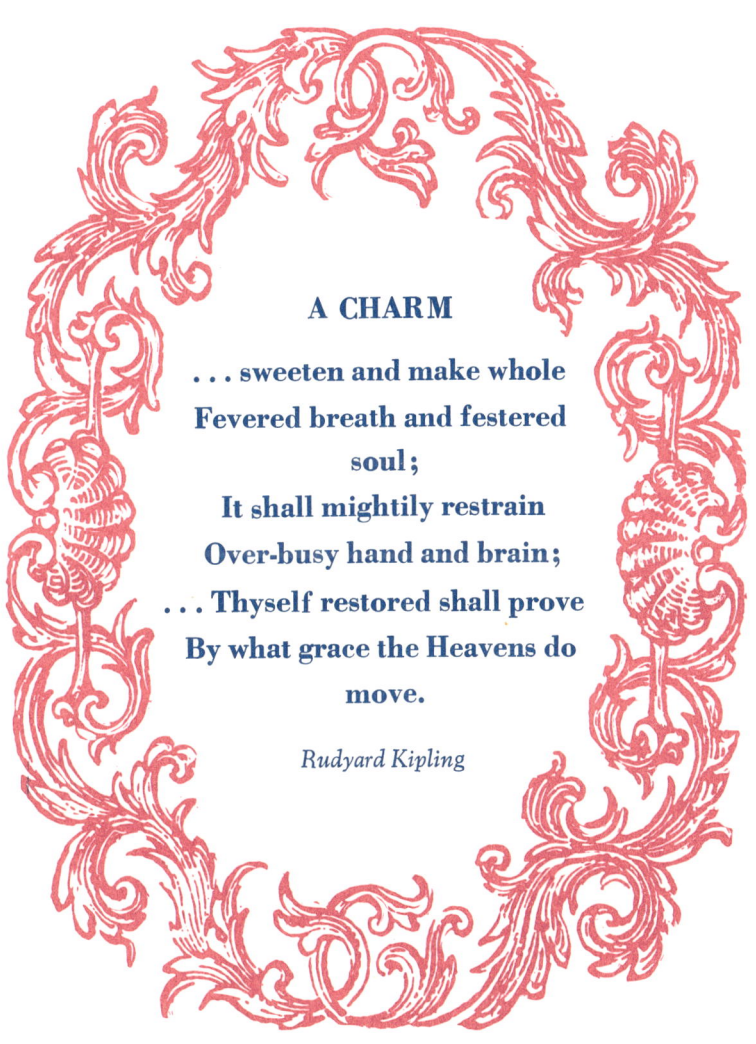

A CHARM

... sweeten and make whole
Fevered breath and festered soul;
It shall mightily restrain
Over-busy hand and brain;
... Thyself restored shall prove
By what grace the Heavens do move.

Rudyard Kipling

Beauty

Lift up thine eyes round about, and behold.

ISAIAH 49:18

MOUNTAIN CHANT OF THE NAVAJO

In beauty may I walk.
All day long may I walk.
Through the returning seasons may I walk.
On the trail marked with pollen may I walk.
With grasshoppers about my feet may I walk.
With dew about my feet may I walk.
With beauty may I walk.

With beauty before me may I walk
With beauty behind me may I walk.
With beauty above me may I walk.
With beauty below me may I walk.
With beauty all around me may I walk.

George W. Cronyn

A single hour of a spring evening is worth
    one thousand pieces of gold;
Flowers send forth scent and the moon is misty;
The notes of the flute from the upper storey
    grow faint,
The swing in the court hangs motionless in the
    night air.

Su Tung-Po

FLOWERS AND MOONLIGHT
ON THE SPRING RIVER

The evening river is level and motionless.
The spring colors just open to their full
Suddenly a wave carries the moon away
And the tidal water comes with its freight of stars.

Yang-Ti.

We thank you, Lord of Heaven,
For all the joys that greet us,
For all that you have given
To help us and delight us
In earth and sky and seas;
The sunlight on the meadows,
The rainbow's fleeting wonder,
The clouds with cooling shadows,
The stars that shine in splendor.
We thank you, Lord, for these.

Jan Struther

Creatures

Let the earth bring forth the living creature after his kind, cattle, and creeping thing, and beast of the earth after his kind.

GENESIS 1:24

PRAYER OF THE OX

Dear God, give me time.
Men are always so driven!
Make them understand that I can never hurry.
Give me time to eat,
Give me time to plod,
Give me time to sleep,
Give me time to think.

Carmen Bernos de Gasztold, translated by Rumer Godden

I call you, my brother,
I call you by your home name which you know well.
If you hear me, come without fear.
The tide runs strongly. The water is so cold.
I am waiting and watching.
Come to me.

Celtic Seal Call

Why do some people talk with such assurance about what they are going to do with the world, as though they owned it when really our share is such a small one? Birds and butterflies, bees and flying insects fill the air; tiny animals climb and burrow and scuttle. And underneath the ground a whole world of life goes on that we never see — moles with grey velvet coats push along, their strong front feet swinging through the earth with a swimmer's breast stroke. Behind them come the groundmice on sly, flying feet, and tucked under a stone is a grey worm, rolled up for the winter. There is myriad life under, on, and above the earth.

Beatrix Potter

LITTLE THINGS

Little things, that run and quail,
And die, in silence and despair!

Little things that fight, and fail,
And fall, on sea, and earth, and air!

All trapped and frightened little things,
The mouse, the coney, hear our prayer!

As we forgive those done to us,
— The lamb, the linnet, and the hare —

Forgive us all our trespasses,
Little creatures, everywhere!

James Stephens

We beseech Thee, O Lord,
to hear our supplication
on behalf of the dumb creation,
who after their kind, bless, praise,
and magnify Thee Forever.
Grant that all cruelty may
cease out of our land and deepen
our thankfulness to Thee for the
faithful companionship of
those whom we delight to call
our friends.

Centenary Prayer
Royal Society for the Prevention of Cruelty to Animals
London

Bird Life

Behold the fowls of the air: for they sow not, neither do they reap, nor gather into barns; yet your heavenly Father feedeth them.

MATTHEW 6:26

PRAYER OF THE LITTLE BIRD

Dear God,
I don't know how to pray by myself
very well,
but will you please
protect my little nest from wind and rain?
Put a great deal of dew on the flowers,
many seeds in my way.
Make your blue very high.
Your branches lissom;
Let your kind light stay late in the sky
and set my heart brimming with such music
that I must sing, sing, sing . . .
Please, Lord.

*Carmen Bernos de Gasztold,
translated by Rumer Godden*

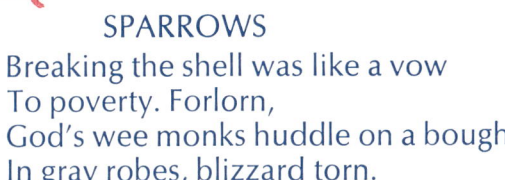

SPARROWS
Breaking the shell was like a vow
To poverty. Forlorn,
God's wee monks huddle on a bough
In gray robes, blizzard torn.

Geraldine Ross

A robin redbreast in a cage
Puts all Heaven in a rage.

William Blake

**Dear Father, hear and bless
Thy beasts and singing birds,
And guard with tenderness
Small things that have no words.**

The Dawn Prayer of the Fisherman

Hearken unto the voice of my cry, my King, and my God: for unto thee will I pray. My voice shalt thou hear in the morning, O Lord;

PSALM 5:2,3

> Fragrant maiden of the sea,
> Thou art full of the graces,
> And the Great White King is with thee.
> Blessed art thou, blessed art thou,
> Blessed art thou, among women;
> Thy breath steering my prayer,
> It will reach the Haven White;
> Let me beseech thy gentle Son
> To whom thou gavest knee and suck
>> To be with us,
>> To be on watch,
>> To be awake;
> To spread over us His Sacred Cowl
> From ray-light to ray-light,
> From the golden-yellow ray of twilight
> To the new-born white ray of dawn,
> And through the dark and dangerous night

To succour us,
To guide us,
To shine on us
With the guidance and glory of the nine rays
    of the Sun,
Through the seas and straits and narrows
Until we come to Moidart
And the Good Clan-Ranald,
O until we come to Moidart
And the Good Clan-Ranald.

Kenneth Macleod

Dear God, be
good to me. The sea
is so wide and my boat
is so small.

Prayer of the Breton Fishermen

God's Son of hosts that none can tell
The fury of the storm repel!
  Dread Lord of the sacrament,
  Save me from the wind's intent,
Spare me from the blast of Hell.

Frank O'Connor

Shepherds and Sheep

Behold the Lamb of God . . . JOHN 1:29

We are his people, and the sheep of his pasture.
PSALM 100:3

SHEEP AND LAMBS

All in the April evening,
April airs were abroad,
The sheep with their little lambs
Passed me by on the road.

The sheep with their little lambs
Passed me by on the road;
All in the April evening
I thought on the Lamb of God.

Up in the blue, blue mountains
Dewy pastures are sweet,
Rest for the little bodies,
Rest for the little feet.

But for the Lamb of God,
Up on the hill-top green,
Only a cross of shame,
Two stark crosses between.

All in the April evening,
April airs were abroad,
I saw the sheep with their lambs
And thought on the Lamb of God.

Katharine Tynan

THE LAMB

Little Lamb, who made thee?
Dost thou know who made thee?
Little Lamb, I'll tell thee;
Little Lamb, I'll tell thee;
He is calléd by thy name,
For he calls himself a Lamb.
He is meek and He is mild;
He came a little child.
I a child, and thou a lamb,
We are calléd by His name.
Little Lamb, God bless thee!
Little Lamb, God bless thee!

William Blake

The Lord is my shepherd; I shall not want.
He maketh me to lie down in green pastures: he leadeth me beside the still waters. He restoreth my soul:
he leadeth me in the paths of righteousness for his name's sake.
Yea, though I walk through the valley of the shadow of death, I will fear no evil: for thou art with me; thy rod and thy staff they comfort me...
Surely goodness and mercy shall follow me all the days of my life: and I will dwell in the house of the Lord for ever.

PSALM 23

Seek ye first the kingdom of God. MATTHEW 6:33

Ask, and it shall be given you;
seek, and ye shall find;
knock, and it shall be opened unto you:
MATTHEW 7:7

I KNOW NOT WHAT I SEEK ETERNALLY

I know not what I seek eternally
on earth, in air, and sky;
I know not what I seek; but it is something
that I have lost, I know not when,
And cannot find, although in dreams invisibly
it dwells in all I touch and see.

Ah, bliss! Never can I recapture you
either on earth, in air, or sky,
Although I know you have reality
and are no futile dream!

The soul that rises with us, our life's star,
Hath had elsewhere its setting,
And cometh from afar:
Not in entire forgetfulness —

Rosalia de Castro. Translated by Muriel Kittel

Bring me my bow of burning gold:
Bring me my arrows of desire:
Bring me my spear; O clouds unfold!
Bring me my chariot of fire.

William Blake

**O God,
give us serenity to accept what cannot be changed,
courage to change what should be changed,
and wisdom to distinguish one from the other.**

Reinhold Niebuhr

O God, Light of the minds that seek Thee,
Life of the souls that love Thee,
and Strength of the thoughts that seek Thee,
enlarge our minds and raise the vision of our hearts
that, with swift wings of thought,
our spirits may reach Thee.

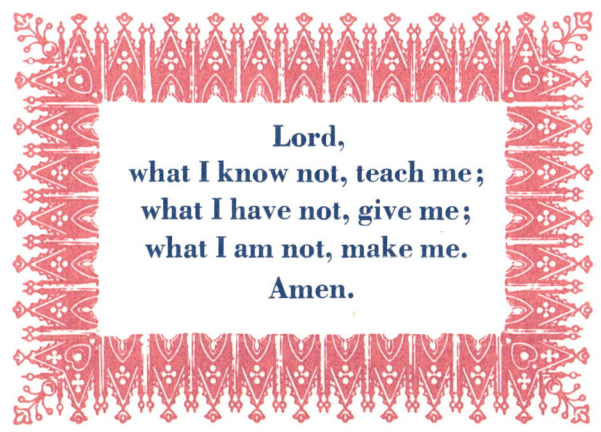

**Lord,
what I know not, teach me;
what I have not, give me;
what I am not, make me.
Amen.**

The Soul's Memories

For thou lovedst me before the foundation of the world. JOHN 17:24

WONDER

How like an Angel came I down!
   How Bright are all Things here!
When first among his Works I did appear
   O, how their Glory me did Crown!
The World resembled his Eternitie,
   In which my Soul did Walk;
And every Thing that I did see,
   Did with me talk.

A Native Health and Innocence
   Within my Bones did grow,
And while my God did all his Glories show,
   I felt a Vigour in my Sense
That was all Spirit. I within did flow
   With Seas of Life, like Wine;
I nothing in the World did know,
   But 'twas Divine. . . .

The Streets were paved with Golden Stones
   The Boys and Girls were mine,
Oh how did all their Lovely faces shine!
   The Sons of Men were Holy Ones.
In Joy, and Beauty, they appear'd to me,
   And every Thing which here I found,
While like an Angel I did See,
   Adorned the Ground.

Thomas Traherne

> The soul that rises with us,
>   our life's star,
> Hath had elsewhere its setting,
> And cometh from afar:
> Not in entire forgetfulness—
>
> *William Wordsworth*

With Thee a moment! then what dreams have play
Traditions of eternal toil arise,
Search for the high austere and lonely way
The Spirit moves in through eternities,
Ah! in the soul what memories arise!

And with what yearning inexpressible,
Rising from long forgetfulness I turn
To Thee, invisible, unrumored, still;
White for Thy Whiteness all desires burn —
Ah! with what longing once again I turn!

A. E.

Prayer

Lord, teach us to pray. LUKE 11:1

O thou that hearest prayer, unto thee shall all flesh come. PSALM 65:2

Master, they say that when I seem
    To be in speech with you,
Since you make no replies, it's all a dream
    — One talker, aping two.

They are half right, but not as they
    Imagine; rather I
Seek in myself the things I meant to say,
    And lo; the wells are dry.

Then, seeing me empty, you forsake
    The listener's role, and through
My dead lips breathe and into utterance wake
    The thoughts I never knew.

And thus you neither need reply
    Nor can; thus, while we seem
Two talking, Thou art One forever, and I
    No dreamer, but thy dream.

C. S. Lewis

O Thou by whom we come to God,
The Life, the Truth, the Way,
The path of prayer Thyself has trod;
Lord, teach us how to pray.

James Montgomery

Grace

*And God is able to make all grace abound
toward you; that ye, always having all sufficiency
in all things, may abound to every good work . . .
Thanks be unto God for his unspeakable gift.*

II CORINTHIANS 9:8,15

Who knows, when raindrops are descending,
   Which thirsty seed will highest grow?
Who knows, when Sabbath knees are bending,
   Where God will greatest grace bestow?

Since it shall rain alike on all —
On ploughland as on stony ground —
Shall any tear unnoticed fall?
Shall any lost sheep not be found?

Who knows what status God has given —
   Who here on earth is small, who great?
Each grass-blade feels the growth of heaven,
   Each raindrop shares the ocean's fate.

Einar Benediktsson

THE PRAYER OF THE DOVE

The Ark waits,
Lord,
The Ark waits on Your will,
and the sign of Your peace.
I am the dove,
simple
as the sweetness that comes from You.
The Ark waits,
Lord;
it has endured.
Let me carry it
a sprig of hope and joy,
and put, at the heart of its forsakenness,
this, in which Your love clothes me,
Grace immaculate.

*Carmen Bernos de Gasztold,
translated by Rumer Godden*

**May Thy grace, O God, be in my eyes
To minister Thy gladness;**

**May Thy grace be in my hands
To minister Thy healing.**

**May Thy grace be in my mind
To minister Thy peace.**

**May Thy grace be in my heart
To minister Thy love.**

Joy

*These things have I spoken unto you,
that my joy might remain in you,
and that your joy might be full.*

JOHN 15:11

JOY TO YOU

Joy to you and gladness,
And that your soul may be
As far away from sadness
As the Star was from the sea
When the Sheep-Boy, the Sheep-Boy,
Heard Heaven's melody.

Smiles to you and laughter,
And also that you may
Be merry the morning after
On good St. Stephen's Day
When the Wren-Boy, the Wren-Boy
Shall sing his roundelay.

Joy to you and gladness,
And that the midnight bell
May ring away the sadness
From the stricken Old Year's knell
When the Chimes-Boy, the Chimes-Boy,
Strikes "Welcome" and "Farewell."

Francis Carlin

**Sing aloud unto God our strength:
make a joyful noise unto the God of Jacob.
Take a psalm, and bring hither the timbrel,
the pleasant harp with the psaltery.
Blow up the trumpet in the new moon,
in the time appointed,
on our solemn feast day.**

PSALM 81:1-3

**O Lord Christ, help us to maintain ourselves in
simplicity and in joy, the joy of the merciful,
the joy of brotherly love. Grant that, renouncing henceforth
all thought of looking back, and joyful with infinite
gratitude, we may never fear to precede the dawn
to praise
and bless
and sing
to Christ our Lord.**

The Rule of Taize

*Holy, holy, holy, is the Lord of hosts:
the whole earth is full of his glory.*

ISAIAH 6:3

CAEDMON'S HYMN

Now we must praise the Ruler of Heaven,
The might of the Lord and His purpose of mind,
The work of the Glorious Father; for He
God Eternal, established each wonder,
He, Holy Creator, first fashioned the heavens
As a roof for the children of earth.
And then our Guardian, the Everlasting Lord,
Adorned this middle-earth for men.
Praise the Almighty King of Heaven.

Between 657 and 680 A.D.

CELTIC RUNE OF PRAISE

    I offer Thee
Every flower that ever grew,
Every bird that ever flew;
Every wind that ever blew,
    Dear God.
Every thunder rolling,
Every church-bell tolling,
Every leaf and sod.
    I offer Thee
Every flake of pure white snow,
Rain and sunshine here below,
Every human joy and woe,
    Dear Lord!
Every river dashing,
Every lightning flashing,
Like an angel's sword.

Holy God, we praise thy Name:
Lord Almighty we confess thee;
All the earth doth thee acclaim
And in awe and wonder bless thee.

Blessings

The Lord bless thee, and keep thee:
The Lord make his face shine upon thee,
and be gracious unto thee:
The Lord lift up his countenance upon thee,
and give thee peace.

NUMBERS 6:24-26

May the road rise with you —
And the wind be always at your back —
And may the Lord hold you in the hollow of His Hand.

From the Gaelic

We pray, not only that our Lord
May bless all that you think and do;
We bless Him with glad heart for what
He hath already wrought in you.

Anonymous

TO WISH YOU
Some new love of lovely things.
Some new forgetfulness of teasing things.
Some higher pride in the praising things.
Some sweeter peace from the hurrying things.
And some closer fence from the worrying things.

John Ruskin

O God, we entrust all who are dear to us
to Thy never-failing care and love, for this
life and the life to come; knowing that Thou art
doing for them better things than
we can desire or pray for.

Book of Common Prayer

L'ENVOI

Go, little book, and wish to all
Flowers in the garden, meat in the hall,
A bit of wine, a spice of wit,
A house with lawns enclosing it,
A living river by the door,
A nightingale in the sycamore!

Robert Louis Stevenson

INDEX

PAGE

79   A CHARM
97   A. E.
30   A family is a single word
11   A PRAYER
32   A QUAKER QUERY
89   A robin redbreast in a cage
83   A single hour of a spring evening
45   A SONG IN TIME OF DEPRESSION
92   All in the April evening
25   And as I was green and carefree, famous among the barns
54   And I said to the man who stood at the gate
27   And Mary said, My soul doth magnify the Lord
46   Andrewes, Lancelot
53, 74, 106   Anonymous
15   Anonymous, 15th century
32   Are you endeavoring to make your home
16   ARMENIAN POEM
35   As the fire under the stone floor
21   At the dawn I seek Thee
14   At the First Supper
65   At the round earth's imagined corners
49   At Tara today in this fateful hour
29   Ausonius

77   Baillie, John
27   Barret, Eaton Stannard
100 Benediktsson, Einar
55   Bestow Thy light upon us, O Lord
70, 89, 93, 95   Blake, William
25   Blessed Lord, what it is to be young
20   Boethius
34, 43, 46, 48, 107   Book of Common Prayer
41   Bowra, C. M.
39   BOY WITH THE CART, THE
20   Bunyan, John
40   Branch, Anna Hempstead
89   Breaking the shell was like a vow
95   Bring me my bow of burning gold

PAGE

104 CAEDMON'S HYMN
102 Carlin, Francis
10 CELESTIAL SURGEON, THE
85 Celtic Seal Call
105 CELTIC RUNE OF PRAISE
87 Centenary Prayer
79 CHARM, A
18 CHRIST-CHILD'S LULLABY, THE
13 Christ keep the Hollow Land
16 Christ took our nature on Him
64, 75 Colum, Padraic
39 I Corinthians 3:8,9,13,14
76 I Corinthians 4:1-2   10 II Corinthians 8:11
61 I Corinthians 15:53-57   100 II Corinthians 9:8, 15
52 II Corinthians 1:7   41 II Corinthians 12:7
45, 64, 82 Cronyn, George W.
55 Crouse, M. Elizabeth

40 DAILY LIVING
90 DAWN PRAYER OF THE FISHERMAN, THE
89 Dear Father, hear and bless
88 Dear God
91 Dear God, be good to me
85 Dear God, give me time
58 DEATH CROON, THE
60 DEATH BE NOT PROUD
94 de Castro, Rosalia
85, 88, 101 de Gasztold, Carmen Bernos
35 Deuteronomy 10:19
48 Deuteronomy 33:27
70 DIVINE IMAGE, THE
60, 65, 75 Donne, John
44 Drake, Sir Francis
11 Drinkwater, John

24 Ecclesiastes 11:9
43 Eliot, T. S.
12 Ephesians 2:10
48 Euripides

110

PAGE

66   EVERLASTING MERCY, THE
33   Exodus 22:21

14   FIRST SUPPER, THE
52   Florio, Giovanni
78   FLOWER, THE
83   FLOWERS AND MOONLIGHT ON THE SPRING RIVER
35   Formosan Prayer
90   Fragrant maiden of the sea
58,106   From the Gaelic
49   From the Old Gaelic
46   Frost, Robert
39   Fry, Christopher

73   Gaelic Hymn
62   Galatians 5:13   70   Galatians 5:22, 23
12   Genesis 1:1
85   Genesis 1:24
28   Genesis 6:2
108 Go, little book
91   God's Son of hosts that none can tell
66   GRACE TO BEGIN AGAIN, THE

47   Habakkuk 2:1
30   Harrington, Helen
54   Haskins, M. L.
15   He came all so still
20   He who would valiant be
66   Heard, Gerald
18   Help us rightly to remember
33   Hebrews 13:2
19   Hebrews 13:14
40,67,71,78   Herbert, George
16   Herrick, Robert
105 Holy God, we praise thy name
58   Home thou'rt going tonight to the Winter Ever-house
78   How fresh, O Lord, how sweet and clean
96   How like an Angel came I down!
12   How was it on that day when from His tower
29   H.T.O.

PAGE

21 I arise from rest with movements swift
50 I bind unto myself this day
85 I call you, my brother
46 I have been one acquainted with the night
94 I KNOW NOT WHAT I SEEK ETERNALLY
105 I offer Thee
34 I saw a stranger yestre'en
42 I will leave man to make the fateful guess
41 I wonder why
10 If I have faltered more or less
82 In beauty may I walk
39 In our fields, fallow and burdened
104 Isaiah 6:3
82 Isaiah 49:18
48 Isaiah 51:22
74 Isaiah 55:6

10 James 1:22
50 Jeremiah 30:10
21 Jewish, 11th century
15 John 1:14   60 John 11:25
92 John 1:29   72 John 14:26
78 John 3:3   102 John 15:11
44 John 4:35   96 John 17:24
54 John 8:12   26 John 20:15
50 Joshua 1:9
102 JOY TO YOU

21 Keble, John
55 Keep Thou my feet
29 Keep us steadfast, O God
19 King of the elements, Love, Father of Bliss
42 I Kings 18:21
79 Kipling, Rudyard
44 Koran, The

93 LAMB, THE
108 L'ENVOI
76 Let me not to the marriage of true minds
47 Let nothing disturb thee

PAGE
98 Lewis, C. S.
46 Lighten our darkness, we beseech Thee, O Lord
93 Little lamb, who made thee?
86 LITTLE THINGS
86 Little things, that run and quail
1   Lord, through this hour
95 Lord, what I know not
49 Lord, when I look upon mine own life
71 Lord, who has form'd me out of mud
67 LOVE
67 Love bade me welcome; yet my soul drew back
29 Love, let us live as we have lived
29 Lowell, James Russell
14 Luke 2:7
17 Luke 2:7   67 Luke 23:34
59 Luke 2:29-30   58 Luke 23:42
72 Luke 5:24   59 Luke 23:46
26 Luke 7:44   26 Luke 24:10
98 Luke 11:1   33 Luke 24:35
17 Luther, Martin

18,19,32,34,38,90   Macleod, Kenneth
27 Magnificat, The
42 MAN TEST
30 Mark 10:14
42 Markham, Edwin
66 Masefield, John
98 Master, they say that when I seem
74 Matthew 5:6
45 Matthew 6:23
42 Matthew 6:24   94 Matthew 7:7
88 Matthew 6:26   28 Matthew 19:5
42,94 Matthew 6:33   35 Matthew 25:38
18 May Christ give to us
106 May the road rise with you
101 May Thy grace, O God, be in my eyes
25 McCord, David
40 MONK IN THE KITCHEN, THE
99 Montgomery, James

113

PAGE
51   Moody, William Vaughn
13   Morris, William
82   MOUNTAIN CHANT OF THE NAVAJO
64   My body restore thou for me
18   My love, my dear, my darling Thou

64   NAVAJO CHANT
52   Negro spiritual
21   New every morning is the love
55, 61 Newman, John Henry
12   Nicholl, Louise Townsend
95   Niebuhr, Reinhold
52   Nobody knows the trouble I've seen
27   Not she with traitorous kiss her Saviour stung
45   Now all my singing Dreams are gone
104   Now we must praise the Ruler of Heaven
106   Numbers 6:24-26

62   O Blessed Trinity
66   O Christ who holds the open gate
66   O forgiving Father
53   O God, Author of the world's joy
95   O God, give us serenity to accept
95   O God, Light of the minds that seek Thee
107   O God, we entrust all who are dear
43   O God, who seest that of ourselves
34   O God, whose blessed Son did manifest himself
41   O God, whose eternal might doth undergird
73   O Holy Spirit of great power
73   O living Christ, make us conscious of thy healing nearness
38   O Loom of Love
103   O Lord Christ, help us to maintain ourselves
77   O Lord of the vineyard, we beg Thy blessing
61   O Lord, support us all the day long
44   O Lord God, when Thou givest to Thy servants
48   O Lord God, who seest that we put not
99   O Thou by whom we come to God
46   O Thou, Light of Lights
91   O'Connor, Frank

PAGE
62   OF SIMPLE SIGNIFICANCE
51   Of wounds and sore defeat
17   OLD CAROL
34   Old prayer
17   Our Little Lord, we give Thee praise
31   Our Father, by whose Name

19   I Peter 2:11
50   Philippians 4:13
86   Potter, Beatrix
11   PRAYER, A
91   Prayer of the Breton Fishermen
101 PRAYER OF THE DOVE, THE
88   PRAYER OF THE LITTLE BIRD
85   PRAYER OF THE OX
90   Psalm 5:2,3
60   Psalm 17:15   92   Psalm 100:3
93   Psalm 23   67   Psalm 103:2,3
78   Psalm 40:3   47   Psalm 116:8
45   Psalm 42:5   54   Psalm 119:105
65   Psalm 51:1,2   32   Psalm 127:1
98   Psalm 65:2   38   Psalm 128:1,2
64   Psalm 71:16   45   Psalm 137:4
103 Psalm 81:1-3   21   Psalm 143:8
39   Psalm 90:17   31   Psalm 144:12

32   QUAKER QUERY, A

21,24,35, Rasmussen, Knud
34   Reveal Thy presence now, O Lord
60   Revelation 1:18
73   Robbins, Howard Chandler
41   Romans 7:18
62   Romans 8:21
89   Ross, Geraldine
15   Rossetti, Christina
51   Rossini, Gioacchino
87   Royal Society for the Prevention of Cruelty to Animals

115

PAGE
103 Rule of Taize, The
34 RUNE OF HOSPITALITY
32 RUNE OF THE PEAT FIRE
49 RUNE OF ST. PATRICK, THE
38 RUNE OF THE WEAVER, THE
107 Ruskin, John

40 Sackville-West, V.
43, 49 St. Augustine
50 St. Patrick
47 St. Theresa
55 Sarum Breviary
44, 76 Shakespeare, William
12 SHAPE CALLED STAR, THE
92 SHEEP AND LAMBS
62 Smallzried, Kay
107 Some new love of lovely things
45 SONG IN TIME OF DEPRESSION, A
89 SPARROWS
86 Stephens, James
10, 18, 108 Stevenson, Robert Louis
14, 84 Struther, Jan
83 Su Tung-po
79 ... Sweeten and make whole

40 Teach me, my God and King
75 Teach me to hear Mermaids singing
52 TEN PAINS OF DEATH, THE
40 The ample busyness of life went by
101 The Ark awaits
83 The evening river is level and motionless
32 The first layer of peats is laid down
35 The lands around my dwelling
16 The lips of the Christ Child
17 The Son of God is born for all
97 The soul that rises with us
71 There is no such thing as humanity
43 There shall always be the Church, and the World
53 These tears that dim my eyes
25 Thomas, Dylan
20 Thou art the comfortable resting-place
43 Thou hast made us for Thyself, O God

PAGE	
55	Thou one all perfect light
71	Thurman, Howard
24	I Timothy 4:12
64	II Timothy 1:1,
29	TO HIS WIFE
70	To Mercy, Pity, Peace, and Love
52	To wait for one who never comes
107	TO WISH YOU
64	TOMORROW I SHALL BEND THE BOW
96	Traherne, Thomas
29	TRUE LOVE
29	True love is but a humble, low-born thing
31	Tucker, F.B.
92	Tynan, Katharine

43	WASTE LAND, THE
87	We beseech Thee, O Lord, to hear our supplication
11	We know the paths wherein our feet should press
106	We pray, not only that our Lord
84	We thank you, Lord of Heaven
1	Westminster Chimes
15	What can I give Him
48	What else is Wisdom
44	What hath this day deserved?
30	WHAT IS A FAMILY?
24	When I was young
51	When to danger duty calls me
73	WHITSUNTIDE
100	Who knows, when raindrops are descending
75	Who reads verse I write
40	Whoever makes a thing more bright
74	Whose is the voice that will not let me rest
86	Why do some people talk with such assurance
44	With him are the keys of the unseen
97	With Thee a moment!
27	WOMAN
96	WONDER
97	Wordsworth, William

83	Yang-ti

117

Acknowledgments

The editor and the publisher have made every effort to trace the ownership of all copyrighted material and to secure permission from copyright holders of such material. In the event of any question arising as to the use of any material the publisher and editor, while expressing regret for inadvertent error, will be pleased to make the necessary corrections in future printings. Thanks are due to the following authors, publishers, publications and agents for permission to use the material indicated.

CYRILLY ABELS, LITERARY AGENT, for excerpt from "Storm At Sea" by Frank O'Connor, copyright © 1959 by Frank O'Connor.

THE CHRISTIAN SCIENCE MONITOR, for "What IS A Family?" by Helen Harrington, copyright © 1961 The Christian Science Publishing Society.

THE CHURCH HYMNAL CORPORATION, for verses from hymns by F. B. Tucker, Ignaz Franz, John Keble and Jan Struther.

CONSTABLE & COMPANY LTD., for "To His Wife" by Ausonius, from *Mediaeval Latin Lyrics* translated by Helen Waddell; for "Flowers and Moonlight on the Spring River" by Yang-ti, from *170 Chinese Poems* translated by Arthur Waley.

COWARD, McCANN & GEOGHEGAN, INC., for "Caedmon's Hymn of Praise," "Celtic Rune of Praise" and "The Grace To Begin Again," from *Diary of Prayer* edited by Elizabeth Goudge.

CURTIS BROWN LTD., for "A Prayer" by John Drinkwater; for "The First Supper" from *A Handful of Pebbles* by Jan Struther; "Take Sky" by David McCord.

DOUBLEDAY & COMPANY, INC., for excerpt from *The Garden* by V. Sackville-West, copyright 1946 by V. Sackville-West; for excerpt from *Rewards and Fairies* by Rudyard Kipling.

HARCOURT BRACE JOVANOVICH, INC., for excerpt from "The Waste Land" in *Collected Poems 1909-1962* by T. S. Eliot, copyright 1936 by Harcourt Brace Jovanovich, Inc., copyright © 1963, 1964 by T. S. Eliot; for "Prayer" from *Poems by C. S. Lewis* edited by Walter Hooper, copyright © 1964 by The Executors of the Estate of C. S. Lewis.

HARPER & ROW, PUBLISHERS, INC., for Formosan Prayer from *The World At One In Prayer* by Daniel J. Fleming, copyright 1942 by Harper & Row, Publishers, Inc.; renewed 1970 by Elizabeth Fleming Smith, E. McClung Fleming and Helen F. Adams.

HOLT, RINEHART AND WINSTON, INC., for "Acquainted With The Night" from *The Poetry of Robert Frost*, edited by Edward Connery Latham, copyright 1928, © 1969 by Holt, Rinehart and Winston, Inc., copyright © 1956 by Robert Frost.

HOUGHTON MIFFLIN COMPANY, for excerpt from a prayer by Boethius; excerpt from "These Tears That Dim"; "The R.S.P.C.A. Centenary Prayer", from *Your Prayers and Mine*, edited by Elizabeth Yates; for excerpt from "Of Wounds And Sore Defeats" from *Selected Poems of William Vaughn Moody*.

MISS ELLA M. JOHNSTON, for selections from *The Road to The Isles* by Kenneth Macleod.

ALFRED A. KNOPF, INC., for "Flowers and Moonlight on the Spring River" by Yang-ti from *Translations from The Chinese* translated by Arthur Waley, copyright 1919, 1941 by Alfred A. Knopf, Inc.; renewed 1947, 1969 by Arthur Waley; for excerpt from "Storm at Sea" from *Kings, Lords and Commoners: An Anthology from The Irish* by Frank O'Connor, copyright © 1959 by Frank O'Connor.

LITTLE, BROWN AND COMPANY, for excerpt from "Take Sky" by David McCord, copyright 1961, 1962 by David McCord.

LIVERIGHT PUBLISHING CORPORATION, for selections from *American Indian Poetry* edited by George W. Cronyn, copyright renewed 1962 by George W. Cronyn.

MACMILLAN PUBLISHING CO., INC., THE MACMILLAN COMPANY OF CANADA LIMITED, MACMILLAN LONDON AND BASINGSTOKE and MRS. IRIS WISE, for "Little Things" from *Collected Poems* by James Stephens, copyright 1926 by The Macmillan Company, renewed 1954 by Cynthia Stephens; Macmillan Publishing Co., Inc. for excerpt from "The Everlasting Mercy": by John Masefield, copyright 1912 by The Macmillan Company, renewed 1940 by John Masefield; Macmillan of London and Basingstoke for selections from *Prayers from The Ark* by Carmen Bernos de Gasztold translated by Rumer Godden.

NEW DIRECTIONS PUBLISHING CORP. and J. M. DENT & SONS LTD., for excerpt from "Fern Hill" from *Collected Poems of Dylan Thomas*, copyright 1946 by New Directions.

OXFORD UNIVERSITY PRESS, for selection from *A Diary of Private Prayer* by John Baillie.

PENDLE HILL, for excerpt from *Mysticism and The Experience of Love* by Howard Thurman (Pendle Hill Pamphlet 115) copyright 1961 by Pendle Hill, Wallingford, Pennsylvania.

DIARMUID RUSSELL AND A. M. HEATH & COMPANY LTD., for "Desire" by A. E.

ST. MARTIN'S PRESS, INC., for "The Shape Called Star" from *World's One Clock* by Louise Townsend Nicholl.

CHARLES SCRIBNER'S SONS, for selection from *A Diary of Private Prayer* by John Baillie, copyright 1949 by Charles Scribner's Sons; for "L'Envoi" and "Christmas Prayer" by Robert Louis Stevenson; for a prayer by Howard Chandler Robbins.

THE SOCIETY OF AUTHORS, for excerpt from *The Everlasting Mercy* by John Masefield; The Society of Authors and Miss Pamela Hinkson for "Sheep and Lambs" by Katharine Tynan.

THE VIKING PRESS, for selections from *Prayers From The Ark* by Carmen Bernos de Gasztold, translated by Rumer Godden, copyright © 1962 by Rumer Godden.

FREDERICK WARNE & CO., INC., for selection from *The Journal of Beatrix Potter from 1881 to 1897*, copyright © 1966 by Frederick Warne & Company, Ltd.

A. P. WATT & SON, MRS. GEORGE BAMBRIDGE, MACMILLAN COMPANY OF LONDON AND BASINGSTOKE, AND THE MACMILLAN COMPANY OF CANADA, LTD., for excerpt from "A Charm" from *Rewards And Fairies* by Rudyard Kipling.

THE WORLD PUBLISHING COMPANY, for poem from *Primitive Song* by C. M. Bowra, copyright © 1962 by C. M. Bowra; for three excerpts from *Beyond The High Hills, A Book of Eskimo Poems* by Knud Rasmussen, copyright 1961 by The World Publishing Company.